THE

GHOSTLY TALES

OF

MICHIGAN'S
HAUNTED
LIGHTHOUSES

Published by Arcadia Children's Books
A Division of Arcadia Publishing
Charleston, SC
www.arcadiapublishing.com

Spooky America is a trademark of Arcadia Publishing, Inc.

First published 2021

Manufactured in the United States

ISBN 978-1-4671-9825-7

Library of Congress Control Number: 2021932535

All images courtesy of Shutterstock; pp.28-29 Craig Sterken/Shutterstock.com.

Spooky America

THE
GHOSTLY TALES
OF
MICHIGAN'S
HAUNTED
LIGHTHOUSES

DIANE TELGEN

Adapted from *Michigan's Haunted Lighthouses* by Dianna Higgs Stampfler

arcadia®
CHILDREN'S BOOKS

CANADA

LAKE
SUPERIOR

7

③

6

8

⑤
①

10

②
9

LAKE
HURON

LAKE
MICHIGAN

4

WISCONSIN

②

3

①

11

④

MICHIGAN

MILWAUKEE ◎

LAKE
ERIE

CHICAGO ◎

12

ILLINOIS

INDIANA

OHIO

①	Soo Locks	**③**	"Graveyard of the Great Lakes"
②	Straits of Mackinac	**④**	Muskegon

TABLE OF CONTENTS & MAP KEY

South Haven Lighthouse

Introduction

How much do you know about lighthouses?

Maybe you've seen one along a lakeshore or ocean coastline, with its bright light warning sailors that land is nearby.

Maybe you know about the special lenses they use to amplify light, called Fresnel lenses. Because they have lots of rings, like a tree, Fresnel lenses can focus light into a tight, narrow beam. In the days before electricity, it was the only way to make lamplight visible from miles away.

Before GPS and radar, sailors had to watch carefully to avoid running aground. In the dark of night, the task became impossible. So how did people keep ships and crew safe from a watery grave?

You guessed it: built lighthouses.

And did you know that ghosts LOVE to haunt lighthouses?

In those days long ago, ships depended on human lighthouse keepers to maintain lamps through the endless dark of night. If you were a keeper, you couldn't take a sick day—or even a quick nap! Not when a single mistake could lead to disaster on the water.

Many lighthouse keepers dedicated their lives—and sometimes their afterlives—to their work. No wonder that lighthouses are some of the most haunted buildings you'll find.

And no state has more lighthouses—more than 120!—than Michigan, the Great Lakes State. That's because it has more freshwater coastline

than any state, province, or *country* on the planet.
Four of the five Great Lakes border Michigan's
two peninsulas. If I told you the state's name
comes from the Algonquian word *Michigama*,
what would you guess it means in English?

That's right: "big lake."

Locals tell spooky legends about more than
thirty of Michigan's lighthouses. Many of the
tales involve former keepers, like the grizzled
Civil War veteran who serves even after death.
Some tell of the families that lived there, like the
widow who took over her husband's post and still
haunts it today. Still, others tell of victims of the
Great Lakes, from sailors lost in shipwrecks to
drowned souls recovered by dutiful keepers.

In these pages, we're going to take a journey
along Michigan's shoreline to visit these haunted
lighthouses. Are their stories just legends? Or are
they real chronicles of the supernatural? Read on
and decide for yourself—*if you dare.*

Fort Gratiot Lighthouse

CHAPTER 1

The Five Phantoms of Fort Gratiot

We're starting our journey on Michigan's east coast, at the southern tip of Lake Huron. There, in the city of Port Huron, at the site of old Fort Gratiot, we'll find Michigan's oldest lighthouse. People have occupied it for almost two hundred years. No wonder there are at least *five* ghosts reported to haunt the building!

That first lighthouse was built in 1825, twelve years before Michigan became the twenty-sixth state. In those days before railroads and automobiles, water provided the easiest way to ship goods. Fort Gratiot guarded the spot where the St. Clair River opened into Lake Huron. Any boats or ships coming from the east had to pass this point. And as more white settlers kept moving west, more traffic sailed past Fort Gratiot. They needed a light to guide their ships and keep them safe.

Of course, many Algonquian-speaking Native Americans, including the Ojibway, Odawa, and Potawatomi tribes, had been navigating Lake Huron for hundreds of years. They hadn't needed a lighthouse because they knew the waters like the back of their hand.

But in the 1800s, white settlers were flocking to Michigan and the other Great Lakes states. Some wanted cheap farmland. Others hoped to make fortunes in timber or mining. Shipping became an important business and needed to be protected. Sailing west with cargo, some captains might never have seen Port Huron before! When that first lighthouse opened in 1825, Colonel George McDougall became its first official keeper.

Back then, military veterans often became keepers. McDougall had served as Michigan's adjutant general—the head of the territory's militias. He also worked as a lawyer. People called him "eccentric" because he often quarreled with judges. Perhaps he was better off living alone at the lighthouse!

McDougall dedicated himself to his work, despite its challenges. That first lighthouse had stairs so narrow that they had to be climbed sideways—and the keeper was a *very* large man. When the hastily built tower collapsed in a storm in 1828, imagine his relief. No more squeezing through its tiny door anymore!

A new lighthouse was constructed at a more visible site north of the fort, and McDougall resumed his duties when it opened in 1830. He served the lighthouse up until he died in 1842, at age seventy-six. Did his death stop him from being eccentric and difficult? No! Right away, people began reporting mysterious sounds coming from both the tower and the keeper's house.

In 2012, the Motor City Ghost Hunters made a trip to the Fort Gratiot Lighthouse, trying to gather evidence of its haunting. They brought motion detectors to alert them to ghostly movements. They had sound and video equipment to document its phantoms. Imagine

being there with them.

You set up your machines and sit down to wait. You know that you and your fellow hunters are the only people in the building . . . the only *living* ones, at least.

Then, all of a sudden, the motion detector goes off! You hear footsteps coming from floor above you! Then a voice mumbles something.

Could it be a ghost?

You pull out your camera to get proof, but it suddenly stops working. You check the battery and the lens, but there's *no reason at all* for it to break down. Then your buddy senses a presence ... they're sure it's a lighthouse keeper!

Is it George McDougall? He'd been dedicated enough to squeeze himself up a narrow staircase and through a tiny door in the first tower. Devoted enough to stay at the second lighthouse until he died. But maybe it's Frank Kimball, the keeper who served the longest.

Kimball had twelve years' experience when he came to Fort Gratiot in October 1894. He served as its head keeper for nearly thirty-four years. In a *Port Huron Times Herald* article from 1927, he'd shared the reasons for his dedication: "You stay a good many years, perhaps because you're foolish."

Foolish enough to stay on even *after death*?

Having dedicated nearly half his life to the Fort Gratiot lighthouse, Kimball died of cancer four years after retiring. He was buried in Saginaw, one hundred miles from the lighthouse. But the Motor City Ghost Hunters are sure they met him during visits in 2013 and 2014. This time, they brought a ghost box. This device uses radio noise to capture electronic voice phenomena. In other words, to listen to ghosts talking!

During those visits, they swept the AM radio band and captured a voice saying, "Kimball." They asked the ghost if he was unhappy that they were trying to contact him. They got only two words in reply.

"I am."

I don't know about you, but if a ghost said I made them unhappy, I'd get out *fast*! I sure wouldn't head into the *basement* of the building it haunted! Especially if the lights started mysteriously turning on and off!

But that's just what these hunters did. After a while, one ghost hunter said he felt a keeper's presence had joined them. And just like that, a sense of calm flooded the room, reassuring everyone.

Maybe Kimball had forgiven them for disturbing his cozy haunting place. Or maybe the calm came from a third keeper, one known for his love of sharing the old lighthouse's history. Robert "Bob" Hanford served in the Coast Guard and came to Fort Gratiot in 1988 as an auxiliary guardsman. His job was to dress up in period costume and give tours to schoolkids and tourists. He loved telling stories about the lighthouse's long—and sometimes spooky— history. Over his twenty years of service, he became known as "Lighthouse Bob."

Lighthouse Bob retired from the lighthouse at age eighty-two and died two years later, in 2010. The Motor City Ghost Hunters claim to have heard from him on several visits. During one particular trip, they saw shadows moving back and forth across an unoccupied room. Next, a water bottle fell off a windowsill, even though no one was anywhere near it. And then, a medium—that's someone who communicates with ghosts— made contact! He called, and a spirit named Bob answered.

Was it "Lighthouse Bob" Hanford? Well, he's the only keeper named Robert or Bob to ever serve at Fort Gratiot. And as a local museum director reported, "He always told me that when people asked if it was haunted, he'd say, 'No, but when I die, I'm going to come back and haunt it.'"

Would *you* want someone to keep a promise like that?

If you're keeping count, that's three of the lighthouse's keepers who are reported to haunt the site. But didn't I say there were as many as five ghosts? So who were the other two?

Well, some tales say that two children haunt the lighthouse area. One was a young girl named

Sarah. The other, a thirteen-year-old boy named Josh, supposedly drowned in a river or lake nearby. We don't have any more details than that, because we haven't found historical documents to connect real people to these stories. But in nearly two hundred years, it's likely the lighthouse has seen many tragic deaths. Sadly, that includes children.

And tragic deaths often lead to ghosts . . .

Fort Gratiot Lighthouse is still operating today, sitting between a public beach and a Coast Guard station. During the summer and fall, you can visit, climb its ninety-four iron stairs, and enjoy the view from the tower.

And maybe, just maybe, you'll hear a ghostly keeper's steps clanging behind you, reminding you to appreciate Michigan's oldest lighthouse.

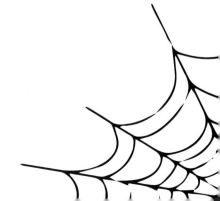

Pointe aux Barques Lighthouse

The Legend of the Lady Keeper

Time to sail north! From Port Huron, it's about seventy-five miles to the tip of Michigan's Thumb area. That's where we'll find our next stop, the Pointe aux Barques Lighthouse—and its resident ghost, the state's first female keeper.

Pointe aux Barques is French for "point of little boats." (Why French? Because the first Europeans to visit the area, more than four hundred years ago, were French fur traders.) The point likely got that name because of its shallow waters—only small boats could navigate them safely. A lighthouse was needed to protect the growing numbers of large cargo ships sailing nearby.

Builders used stone taken from the Lake Huron shore to construct both the tower and the keeper's quarters. On March 6, 1848, Peter Loren Shook became its first keeper. He moved his wife, Catherine and their eight children into the small, one-story keeper's quarters.

A year later, tragedy struck the family. Catherine got sick, and Peter went to fetch a doctor. Dr. John Heath came and treated her and then stayed for dinner. But when the family offered to let him stay the night, he passed. A storm was approaching, and he had more patients to see early the next morning. And so Peter took Dr. Heath back to town by boat.

The two men would never be seen again.

We can only guess what happened, since their bodies were never recovered. The storm would have swamped their small boat, so the men likely drowned after it capsized. A newspaper reported that their boat was later found on a beach—fifty miles away!

Poor Catherine! After the tragic loss of her husband, how would she support eight children without him? Luckily, the US Lighthouse Service offered to let her take her husband's place as keeper. With a home and Catherine's $350 annual salary, her family was saved—and she became Michigan's first female keeper.

But Catherine's problems didn't end there. Less than three months after losing her husband, a chimney fire destroyed the keeper's house and most of the family's belongings. She suffered burns while trying to prevent the fire from spreading. A new residence wouldn't be built until 1857, so she and her family had to live in temporary quarters. Still, she continued her keeper's duties, tending the light until she resigned in 1851.

Catherine Shook faced many challenges, and she was only fifty when she died in 1860. With so much loss and suffering, is it any wonder she's haunted the area ever since? Countless people claim to have seen a woman's ghost wandering the Pointe aux Barques residence and grounds.

Sometimes she's wearing a full-length white gown. Sometimes she's dressed all in black, as if she were still in mourning for her husband. Sometimes she's wearing an apron and looking out the window, her ghost claiming the rebuilt home she never got to enjoy while alive.

But visitors don't just see ghostly visions. People have also heard footsteps echoing in the lighthouse tower, clanging on its beautiful spiral staircase. They've smelled pipe tobacco when no one in the area is smoking. And they've felt sudden cold spots—which supernatural experts consider a sign of ghostly activity—in the historic house.

One local paranormal group visited the keeper's quarters with a ghost box, hoping to capture a ghostly voice. While they were setting up in the living room, they suddenly heard something being moved across the floor above their heads. They slowly crept up the stairs. What could be making those loud scraping sounds?

When they entered the room, they found the source of a noise: an empty rocking chair sat two feet away from where it had been when they last checked it.

It was still rocking!

Had Catherine Shook's ghost suddenly left the chair—or was she *still there*, invisibly rocking?

I sure wouldn't stick around to find out!

The Pointe aux Barques Lighthouse still warns boats on Lake Huron away from the coast. This makes it one of the oldest continuously operating lights on the Great Lakes. Today, the Coast Guard maintains the facility, using remote control to monitor its automated beacon.

You can still visit the tower, however. A local historical society has restored it with artifacts from its early days—including a 1,400-pound Fresnel lens that dates to 1873. You'll also find a museum in the former keeper's residence.

While you're there, it should be easy to imagine what lighthouse life was like in the nineteenth century for Michigan's first female lighthouse keeper. Look out the window at the lake. And maybe Catherine Shook's ghost, seeking the peace that often escaped her in life, will join you.

Saginaw River Rear Range Lighthouse

CHAPTER 3

The Eerie Rear Range Light Ghost

From Pointe Aux Barques, we're going to head west and travel into Saginaw Bay. We'll sail to the end, where Bay City sits at the mouth of the Saginaw River. That's where we'll find the Saginaw River Rear Range Light. This lighthouse has been tied to the Brawn family since its earliest days—and people say a Brawn still haunts the place!

But exactly what kind of lighthouse is a "rear range light," anyway? If you guessed that it's found near a "front range light," you're right! Range lights always come in pairs, to help ships steer a precise course.

You've probably noticed that when you're moving in a car or boat, fixed objects like buildings change position as you go by. Their placement—left, right, ahead, behind—depends on your viewpoint. Range lights use this trick of perspective to keep you on the right heading. They're placed so that if ships get the two range lights to line up, one on top of the other, they'll be on the right path.

Back in the 1800s, more and more people sailed to Bay City, a port which shipped local timber all around the Great Lakes. The port's first lighthouse opened in 1841, consisting of a 62-foot-tall stone tower and keeper's house. In 1866, the Brawn family—the keeper, Peter; his wife, Julia; and their youngest child, sixteen-year-old DeWitt—moved there.

Not long after the Brawns moved in, Peter became so ill he had to stay in bed. Julia took over his duties at the lighthouse, assisted by her son. When Peter died in 1873, his widow became the official keeper at the lighthouse, but DeWitt also played an important role.

Engineers had dredged the river, allowing more traffic to pass in and out of the bay. The lighthouse needed an upgrade, and that's when DeWitt suggested the idea of range lights. They built the front light eight hundred feet away from the original lighthouse. They placed the rear light almost half a mile to the southwest, further along the river. The new light system opened in 1876, with Julia Brawn as its official keeper. Her new home stood next to the rear range light.

Around this time, Julia married again, to a man named George Way. Back then, society preferred men to be in charge of things, so Julia was demoted to assistant keeper in 1877, while George became head keeper. Five years later, they abolished the office of assistant keeper altogether, ignoring Julia's hard work. How unfair!

Tall ships in Bay City, Michigan

To make things worse, in May 1883, they restored the assistant keeper position and gave it to her grandson Leonidus Charlton! So when George Way died that October, Julia—no longer

a lighthouse employee—was forced to leave her home. Once again, Julia's years of dedication of refilling the lamp's oil three or four times every night were overlooked!

If all your hard work had been disrespected and you'd been kicked out of your house, you'd probably feel like haunting the place after you died. And after Julia Brawn Way died in 1889, locals say that's exactly what happened. Since then, people have heard footsteps on the tower's spiral steel staircase, even when no one else is there.

One particularly spooky story dates to 1980. By this time, the range lights had been under Coast Guard control for forty years. One night, a Guardsman had just gone to bed in the old keeper's quarters when the lookout on duty awakened him in the deep dark of night. The younger man had heard footsteps going up and down the empty tower, and he didn't want to investigate by himself.

The two men checked all the doors.

All of them were locked. Yet the sound of footsteps still echoed around them as they continued to explore. Then they spotted it: an uncanny glow from one side of the tower. The range lights had been switched off in the 1960s, after the channel into the river had been widened. The moon shone on the opposite side of the tower, away from the glow. So what could cause that eerie light?

The younger Guardsman suggested they report the incident to headquarters. But the older one said, "No way! The last thing I want is to be called on the carpet before a bunch of officers in Detroit asking about a ghost!" He didn't want his superiors thinking he'd been seeing things. Military handbooks don't admit there are such things as ghosts.

But *we* know better, don't we?

Had Julia Brawn Way's ghost caused the strange sounds and eerie lights the Guardsmen witnessed? Her work as a keeper was dismissed during her lifetime. Maybe haunting the lighthouse is her way of demanding we recognize her.

The Coast Guard sold the property not long after this story, and it fell into disrepair. Since then, the Saginaw River Marine Historical Society has worked to restore the rear range light. While the tower gets opened for special occasions, they hope someday to make it a regular tourist attraction.

Perhaps when that happens, you can go visit. Maybe Julia Brawn Way will keep you company as you take a tour, with her ghostly steps reminding you that female keepers deserve respect!

Old Presque Isle Lighthouse

CHAPTER 4

The Protective Specter of Old Presque Isle

Time to head back out to Lake Huron and enjoy a long day of sailing. It's about 150 miles to our next stop, at the northeast tip of Michigan's mitten. Along with one of the oldest lighthouses on Lake Huron, where we'll find some very spooky stories!

In French, Presque Isle means "almost an island," and that's a good description of this peninsula. This finger of land needed a lighthouse to keep ships safe as they sailed into the harbor. So the young state of Michigan built one in 1840.

But the lighthouse was small: only eighteen feet in diameter and thirty feet tall. It's no surprise that after thirty years, they replaced it with a taller tower and a set of range lights. The old lamp was taken away, and the windows were boarded up. The old lighthouse sat neglected, even after someone bought the property to use as a private park. By 1930, its roof had collapsed, and its brick-and-stone walls were crumbling.

That's when Francis Stebbins purchased the property. He replaced the century-old keeper's house with a new cottage, but he ignored the old lighthouse. When visitors kept asking to tour the old tower, he decided to fix it up and create a museum. By 1965, he had even installed a Fresnel lens.

Not long after, Stebbins received bad news. The Coast Guard told him he couldn't turn on his light because it might interfere with the official navigation lights and confuse sailors. Remember that detail: no lights allowed in the old tower!

Still, the museum became a success. In 1972, Stebbins hired a retired couple, George and Lorraine Parris, to serve as live-in caretakers.

They loved hosting tourists and telling them all about Presque Isle's history. After George died from a heart attack in 1992, Lorraine stayed on the job at the lighthouse.

And that's when the spooky stuff started to happen.

Not long after George's death, Lorraine was driving home to the lighthouse. As she got close, she saw a fuzzy white light near the tower. But she knew the lighthouse lamp couldn't be lit. The tower didn't even have electricity!

At first, Lorraine thought her eyes were fooling her. But over the next three weeks, the glowing white light kept reappearing. She finally asked the Coast Guard if they had turned on the power.

They hadn't.

"Well, you know what?" she told the Guardsmen. "It has to be my husband, George. He has come back to tell me he is still watching over me."

And George certainly does that! One stormy evening, Lorraine got ready to leave the museum

Old Presque Isle Lighthouse

after a day of giving tours. But when she tried the handle of the cottage door, it was stuck—like someone on the other side was holding it shut.

Just then, lightning flashed through the air, and a huge rumble of thunder shook the cottage. Lorraine decided to wait for the storm to pass. When she finally tried the door again, it opened easily. She walked out to her car and couldn't believe what she saw.

A large patch of grass had been scorched black by lightning!

If Lorraine had left the cottage on her first try, she might have been electrocuted!

Yet Lorraine wasn't upset. Instead, she felt comforted. George's ghost was still watching over her.

Lorraine isn't the only one who has seen signs of George's ghost, however. The mysterious tower light has been spotted from all directions. In fact, so many people out sailing or fishing have seen it that the Coast Guard came to investigate it. They could find no explanation.

No *earthly* explanation, that is.

The Old Presque Isle Lighthouse is now owned by the local township and managed by a nonprofit museum society. During the tourist season, you can visit the 1870 lighthouse and range lights and the 1905 Keeper's House Museum.

Just watch out, for rumors say George's ghost likes to visit kids. One time, a girl climbed into the lighthouse tower by herself. She came down giggling, so her mom asked her what was so funny.

"I was talking to the lighthouse keeper up in the lighthouse," she said.

Her mother replied, "There's no lighthouse keeper."

"Yes, there is, look up there!" The little girl pointed to a picture. "There he is, he's the one who made me laugh!"

It was a picture of George Parris.

So go ahead, climb the tower of the Old Presque Isle Lighthouse. Just be prepared for a ghost to haunt you step … by step … by step.

Point Iroquois Lighthouse

CHAPTER 5

The Tragic Ghosts of Point Iroquois

It's time to head to Lake Superior. This greatest of the Great Lakes has earned its name, as it's the largest freshwater lake on the planet. We'll sail straight north from Old Presque Isle and then round the eastern tip of the Upper Peninsula before entering the St. Marys River.

There's just one little problem: rapids! Three-quarters of a mile long and twenty-two feet high, they block the mouth of the St. Marys.

Luckily for us, engineers built the St. Marys Fall Canal, also known as the Soo Locks. Before the first canal was built in 1855, the rapids made it impossible to sail between Lakes Huron and Superior. When it opened, the canal used two locks—closed chambers where you can raise or lower water levels—to help boats navigate the difference in elevation.

Today, the canal has four giant locks that allow huge cargo ships to travel the Great Lakes. And once we've followed them into Lake Superior, we'll soon find Point Iroquois, right before the lake starts widening into Whitefish Bay. The ghosts here reveal the dangers found in the wilds of the Upper Peninsula.

The point gets its name from a famous battle in 1662. It pitted invaders from the Iroquois Confederacy against the local Chippewa tribe (also known as the Ojibwa). The Chippewa emerged the victors, and their descendants still live in towns and cities throughout the Upper Peninsula.

Point Iroquois became an important landmark for the growing traffic on Lake Superior. The first lighthouse, a simple wooden structure, began operating in 1857. It was replaced by a brick tower in 1870. But despite the improvements, the lighthouse couldn't prevent all disasters on the lake.

And that's where the ghosts come in.

In November 1919, a huge snowstorm blew across the lake and struck the steamship *Myron*. The ship was towing a barge that held more than two thousand tons of lumber. (That weighs as much as five hundred hippos or one thousand cars!) When the blizzard hit, Captain Walter Neal decided to abandon the barge. But as sixty-mile-per-hour winds continued pounding the *Myron*, giant waves swamped the ship, flooding the engines.

Without power, the crew had to abandon the sinking ship. While seventeen men scrambled for the lifeboats, Captain Neal remained in the pilothouse, following the tradition that a captain always goes down with his ship. But miraculously, his fragment of the ship stayed afloat while the rest of the *Myron* sank. Captain Neal was rescued the next day.

Would-be rescuers found some of the crew a few days later. They were still in the lifeboat, still wearing their life jackets, but they had *all* frozen to death. Then five more lost souls were discovered—encased in ice—near Whitefish Point. It was next spring before the last of the seventeen victims could be recovered.

Their bodies had to be chopped from the frozen waters of Lake Superior.

These men were buried not far from Point Iroquois, with a memorial to the *Myron* marking their graves. Many stories say the frozen crew haunt the shoreline next to the lighthouse. And why wouldn't they? Imagine your body being lost in the frigid ice of Lake Superior for months on end—your spirit would certainly seek the warmth and protection of the lighthouse.

This isn't the only terrible tale involving the Point Iroquois Lighthouse, however. Once, after a psychic visited the tower, she told a volunteer working there that she sensed the spirit of a child. A little girl, to be exact.

The psychic's words "made the hair on the back of my neck stand up," the volunteer remarked. That's because the story reminded her of a local tragedy that made national news back in 1948.

On that dreadful day, three-year-old Carol Ann Pomranky was playing on the porch of the family cabin. (They lived near the lighthouse in Marquette National Forest. It's now known as Hiawatha National Forest.) Suddenly, a black bear emerged from the forest and snatched the little girl. By the time her mother could summon help, it was too late. Hunters tracked and killed the bear, but poor Carol Ann had already died.

So why would her ghost end up at the Point Iroquois Lighthouse? As the volunteer explained, spirits often haunt places that "made a big impression on them" when they were alive. For tiny Carol Ann, "seeing the massive tower with her family would have been very impressive."

Thankfully, that was likely the last time a bear killed anyone in Michigan. So don't worry about bear attacks when you visit the Point Iroquois Lighthouse. Its lamp was replaced by an automatic light in 1962, but the lighthouse and

keeper quarters have been preserved for tourists. The seventy-two-step climb up the tower will bring you to a magnificent view of Lake Superior.

If you walk along the beach, perhaps a lost crewman of the *Myron* will join you, still hoping for warmth and safety. Or a little ghost girl might tap your hand, looking for a playmate and reminding you to admire the magnificent Point Iroquois Lighthouse.

Marquette Harbor Lighthouse

CHAPTER 6

The Red-Headed Wraith of Marquette Harbor

Good thing the weather looks fine, because we have 150 miles to sail before we reach our next haunted lighthouse. It's located in the largest city in the Upper Peninsula, founded during the iron-ore boom. It started as New Worcester in 1849, but within a year, it had been renamed in honor of the French missionary and explorer Jacques Marquette. There, we'll find a lighthouse famed for the number of children who have lived there—including a ghost girl!

Marquette quickly became an important port for shipping iron ore, so they needed a light to guide cargo ships. The first lighthouse was built in 1853 on a cliff overlooking the harbor. But shoddy construction meant it soon needed to be replaced. In 1866, the new forty-foot-tall tower, made of brick, began operating. They also built a keeper's quarters, and at first, one keeper could handle the job.

But between 1874 and 1875, the Lighthouse Board added a fog signal. Then they installed a breakwater wall with a light at the end of the point. That required an assistant lighthouse keeper, who lived in their own private quarters. So over the years, quite a few families made the Marquette Harbor Lighthouse their home. Perhaps that's why today, locals swear they've seen ghostly kids playing on the grounds.

Stories tell of a young girl's ghost who likes to haunt the upper floor of the lighthouse. The spirit is barefoot and wears an old-fashioned dress, maybe from the early 1900s. She seems to enjoy the company of mothers and other children. One witness commented, "Lots of times, you'll hear her skipping around the lighthouse and hear giggles," but nobody's there!

Several locals believe this young ghost girl, who has red hair and green eyes, is named Jesse. Sometimes she's found staring out at Lake Superior, especially on days when the waters are

calm. Is she waiting for the return of someone who never came home?

So who could this ghostly child be? One of the keepers of the original lighthouse, Nelson Truckey, had a son named Jesse. He was five years old when his father began serving as keeper in 1861 and nine when the family left. His mother, Eliza, also served as an official keeper when her husband left to fight for the Union in the Civil War. But Jesse lived in the wrong time period and is the wrong gender to match our ghost.

Maybe it's one of the children of Bill and Catherine McGuire, who came to Marquette as keepers in 1884. They lived at the lighthouse year-round, and Bill McGuire's records mention his children. In winters, they skated in the frozen harbor and enjoyed cozy Christmases in their lighthouse home. The family's ten-year stay also included the horrible storms of 1887. That year, they had to keep the fog signals wailing for a record 697 hours—that's 29 days straight! But we can't verify the names of the McGuire children, and that time period isn't quite right either.

So perhaps our ghost was the daughter of Robert Carlson, who served as keeper from 1898 to 1903. She's the right age—she was six when the family moved into the lighthouse—but her name was Cecilia, which doesn't sound anything like Jesse.

There are stories of a keeper's daughter who suffered a serious injury during the early 1900s. Could she be our mystery spirit?

Or is the ghost connected to an incident in 1927? That year, six-year-old Robert Carlson was playing on the rocks and fell into the lake. Luckily, a quick-acting Coast Guardsman saw him fall. He rescued and revived the boy, who made a full recovery. But this Robert Carlson was too young to be Cecilia's brother and too old to be her son. And not a girl named Jesse, in any case!

We may never know which real-life child haunts the Marquette Harbor Lighthouse. Not everyone's story gets saved in historical records. Sometimes, all that remains are legends—and the ghosts! Our red-headed spirit is not only a reminder of all the children who spent happy childhoods living at the lighthouse, but also of those whose lives may have ended tragically or too soon.

Today, the Coast Guard maintains the light, but the keeper's quarters and surrounding grounds are a museum and public park. Famed

for the bright red paint it's worn since 1965, the lighthouse has become a highlight for visitors to Marquette.

You can tour the lighthouse and grounds during the summer months, and who knows? Maybe Jesse will appear at your shoulder as you look out the lighthouse window. You could solve the mystery and ask Jesse to tell her tragic story.

If you're brave enough to talk to a ghost, that is.

Big Bay Point Lighthouse

The Restless Spirit of Big Bay Point

Back to Lake Superior, heading northwest! We've only got thirty miles before we reach our next destination. It's not as old as some of the other places we've visited, but some still consider it the most haunted lighthouse in Michigan. It certainly has one of the most tragic histories you'll find on our trip.

The Big Bay Point Lighthouse opened in 1896, three years after the US Congress approved its construction. It sat midway between Marquette and Keweenaw Bay, along an unlighted stretch of shore where the land began to curve. Many ships had been wrecked along Big Bay Point, so the new light needed an experienced keeper—H. William Prior.

Prior dedicated himself to his work, and he expected the same level of care from his assistants. Unfortunately, that's not what he got, as you can read in the records he kept. He wrote of his first assistant, Ralph Heater, he "has not the energy to carry him down the hill and if I speak to him about it he makes no answer, but goes on just as if he did not hear me." Heater later claimed he could not work because of a bad back, even though he could walk the thirty-three miles to Marquette. Prior soon got approval to get rid of Heater.

The next assistant, George Beamer, soon left to fight in the Spanish-American War. His wife, Jennie, filled in as assistant, and Prior wrote no complaints about her work. But when George Beamer returned from war, he too complained of a bad back. Prior wrote, "Asst. Beamer complains of being sick and talks of leaving the station to go home to Detroit. He is too high strung for a light keeper's asst, between himself and his wife this season I imagine that I am keeping a Home for the Helpless Poor instead of a U.S. Lighthouse."

Prior got approval to transfer Beamer out, but the next assistant only lasted six months. After four years of second-rate help, the head keeper decided to keep it in the family. He hired his nineteen-year-old son George as assistant. And for a year, the arrangement worked.

Then tragedy struck.

Footing can be tricky out by the water, especially when waves pound the shore. One day, George slipped on the steps out near the lighthouse landing. He gashed his leg so badly, you could see his shinbone. On April 16, 1901, the official keeper's record noted, "George E. Prior is very lame today. I will take him to Marquette tomorrow."

The record from two days later reads, "He will have to remain in hospital for treatment having been hurt by falling on steps on [the landing] crib."

In fact, the tissue in George's leg had started to die, due to a condition called gangrene. Medicines to treat infections hadn't been invented yet. So a bad wound could fester—that means putrefy or rot—even though you were still alive! Doctors could amputate a limb with gangrene, but sometimes the infection had already spread into your blood. And then you were a goner.

The station entry for June 13, 1901, simply said, "1.30 pm Keeper summoned to Marquette to bury his son who died this morning."

H. William Prior's last entry in the lighthouse logbook was dated two weeks later, just noting "general work." The next day, June 28, he vanished. Some locals said they saw him headed into the forest with his gun and some poison. But a search turned up nothing. That fall, his wife and remaining four children moved away.

In November 1902, a local hunter made a

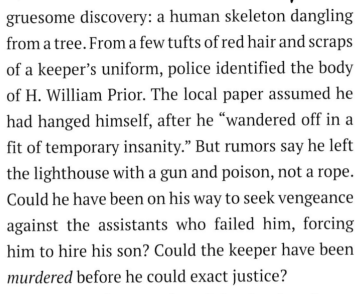

gruesome discovery: a human skeleton dangling from a tree. From a few tufts of red hair and scraps of a keeper's uniform, police identified the body of H. William Prior. The local paper assumed he had hanged himself, after he "wandered off in a fit of temporary insanity." But rumors say he left the lighthouse with a gun and poison, not a rope. Could he have been on his way to seek vengeance against the assistants who failed him, forcing him to hire his son? Could the keeper have been *murdered* before he could exact justice?

Whatever happened to Prior in that forest, his restless spirit now haunts the Big Bay Point Lighthouse. The stories started in the late 1980s, after the property was converted into a bed and breakfast by Buck and Marilyn Gotschall and his wife. One of the first guests reported seeing a ghostly figure wearing a lighthouse service uniform.

This was just the first of several reports of a tall, red-headed man roaming the property, wearing an old-fashioned keeper's uniform. Plus, there are windows and doors that seem to open and close by themselves, lights that mysteriously switch on, and footsteps on wooden floors when nobody's there . . .

Buck Gotschall was certain the ghost belonged to Prior. "Every morning in the spring he wakes me up, taps me lightly and bids me to go fishing," he said. "I always try to comply. I don't want a mad ghost around."

One of the property's next owners, Linda Gamble, is also convinced she met Prior's ghost. Late one night, she heard doors opening in the kitchen. "I stormed up, but no one was there," she recalled. "So I figured it must be Will, and I said . . . 'I have to get up in the morning and make breakfast, so cut it out.' Then I slammed a cupboard and went back to bed."

The next morning, *all the open cupboard doors had been closed.* Linda never heard the ghost again. Maybe he thought a "No Vacancy" sign could also apply to hauntings and didn't want to be kicked out!

But guests still claim to see spooky reflections of a person dressed in old keeper's clothes behind them in the mirror. Others report waking up in the middle of the night to find a ghostly figure at the foot of their bed, *watching them.*

The Big Bay Point Lighthouse is still a bed and breakfast. (Sadly, they don't allow pets or kids to stay there.) But during the summer, you can take a tour, visit the tower, and see the restored Fresnel lens. People tells stories of sailors lost in nearby shipwrecks who like to wander the area, so maybe you'll see one of these ghosts on the grounds.

Or when you're old enough, you can stay overnight at the bed and breakfast, if you dare. Even if it's years from now, you may see the spirit of Big Bay's tragic keeper.

After all, H. William Prior's ghost has been haunting the place for more than 120 years, so what's a few more?

Whitefish Point Lighthouse

The Storm-Tossed Specters of Whitefish Point

But now it's time to turn around and sail back toward the Lower Peninsula. Along the way, we'll hit the most dangerous stretch of water in the Great Lakes. For 80 miles, between Munising and Whitefish Point, there's no safe harbor to protect from Lake Superior's deadly storms. Along this "Graveyard of the Great Lakes," historians say you can find 200 of the 550 ships the lake has claimed.

Whitefish Point juts into Lake Superior just where the lake begins to narrow and approach the

St. Marys River. It's so important for navigation that it boasts Superior's oldest operating lighthouse, completed in 1849. It was rebuilt in 1861 with a seventy-six-foot tower, which could be seen by all ships entering the bay from the Soo Locks.

Despite the reliable light marking the shore, there were still other dangers on the lake. In 1853, the *Independence* sank after its boiler exploded. Collisions took the *Comet* in 1875 and the *Osborn* in 1884. The *Isaac M. Scott* and *John B. Cowles* both sank in 1909 after they crashed into each other. A storm swallowed the *Niagara* in 1897.

But the most famous shipwreck along this stretch of water was the iron-ore carrier *Edmund Fitzgerald*, which sank with all crew on November 10, 1975. It was memorialized the following year in the number-two hit single "The Wreck of the *Edmund Fitzgerald*."

And these are only some of the lives and ships lost off of Whitefish Point!

With so many tragic losses nearby, it's only natural that ghosts flock to the Whitefish Point Lighthouse. Some people have reported seeing a phantom ship, a gray schooner with full sails, disappearing into nothing. Sailing superstition says that ghost ships like these are doomed to forever reenact their losses on the lake. Perhaps this phantom is the *Invincible*, the first schooner to be built for Lake Superior shipping—and the first ship to wreck near Whitefish Point, in 1816.

Most of the ghost sightings here have been at the lighthouse and in the crew's quarters, which now has five rooms available for overnight stays. The story of one sighting comes from a guest who visited in 2008. As she slept, a stroking sensation on her face startled her awake. The gentle touch felt like how a parent would caress their child, so she went back to sleep. But at 6:00 a.m., her closed, *locked* door suddenly popped open!

The woman got up and saw no one in the hallway, so she explained it away as air currents.

Then she talked to two guests who were staying on another floor. For two days straight, their door had suddenly opened ... *at exactly 6:00 a.m.*!

Not only that, one of them had felt someone stroking their back in the middle of the night! The other glimpsed the shadowy figure of a man in a blue uniform near their bathroom door. That sure sounds like a ghost to me!

I'd be too scared to investigate Whitefish Point any further, but spooky images and phantom footsteps are just what ghost hunters hope to find. One group braved the haunted lighthouse to set up their video camera. They captured a woman's voice, even though they were the only two people in the building.

The only two *living* people, at least!

Another group of ghost hunters had their own spooky encounters. Their equipment recorded all the classic signs of supernatural activity: weird electromagnetic (EMF) signals, mysteriously drained batteries, and tripped motion sensors. Their thermometers also registered unexplained cold spots, more sure evidence of ghosts.

Nevertheless, they stayed overnight in the crew quarters. That's when one person discovered their pajamas had been *moved* from one end of the bed to the other. I'm sure they didn't sleep very well . . . especially when the phantoms kept *touching* them during the night!

One psychic visitor claims there are at least fifty spirits haunting Whitefish Point! They include a woman in 1890s dress who stares from the tower out into the lake, a Native American girl who wanders through various buildings, and a young girl in an old-fashioned dress who drifts around—this ghost girl was even caught on tape in an upstairs bedroom. In fact, a staff member recalls sitting on a bed in the crew quarters when she felt a gentle touch on her arm. When she looked over, she found a dented spot on the bed next to her, *exactly the size of a small child*!

So many people have been lost along this stretch of shore that it's hard to figure out who all these ghosts could be. Lifesaving patrols used to find bodies washed ashore after every big storm—sometimes even encased in winter ice! Many of them are buried in unmarked, unrecorded graves.

But the woman in 1890s dress could have been a keeper's wife or someone waiting for a sailor who would never return from the lake. The Native American girl might have been from one of the Anishinabek tribes that dominated the area before Europeans arrived. (Their descendants, including the Chippewa, or Ojibwa, still live in the Upper Peninsula.) And the little girl ghost? One psychic thinks she was Bertha Endress, the granddaughter of keeper Robert Carlson.

We met the Carlsons at the Marquette Harbor Lighthouse and wondered whether Robert's daughter Cecilia had any connection to the ghost found there. In 1903, the Carlson family moved from Marquette to Whitefish Point, and Cecilia grew up there and got married. But she divorced her husband and later became ill, so her daughter Bertha, born in 1910, often lived at the lighthouse with her grandparents. Bertha eventually worked to help establish the museum there. So perhaps her spirit remains there, continually looking after her childhood home.

On your visit to Whitefish Point, you can tour the Great Lakes Shipwreck Museum and see physical artifacts from the area's many wrecks. And if you dare, stay overnight in the old crew's quarters. Maybe you'll be awoken in the middle of the night by a ghostly touch on your cheek. You might glimpse a phantom ship, sailing through an uncanny mist. When it comes to Lake Superior's dangers, there's no shortage of eerie reminders here!

Good thing we're heading back south. But beware—Michigan's west coast is just as spooky as the rest of the state . . .

Waugoshance Lighthouse

CHAPTER 9

The Prankster Poltergeist of Waugoshance

We've sailed our way back through the Soo Locks, around the tip of the Upper Peninsula, and are heading west on Lake Huron. Once we pass through the Straits of Mackinac (pronounced *MACK-in-awe*), we'll be in Lake Michigan!

Fun fact: Lake Huron and Lake Michigan are actually two parts of one giant body of water! They're connected by the Straits, which allow water levels on both sides to remain equal. Even at their narrowest point, where the mighty

Mackinac Bridge connects the Upper and Lower Peninsulas, the Straits are still five miles wide. But early European settlers didn't have satellite maps. Instead of one big lake, they saw two, so now we have Lakes Michigan and Huron.

And once we reach the western end of the Straits, there we'll find our next haunted stop: the Waugoshance Shoal Lighthouse. Opened in 1851, it was the first lighthouse on the Great Lakes to be completely surrounded by water. That's where the *shoal* part comes in—a shoal is a submerged ridge of land that can prove dangerous to ships. Without a signal at Waugoshance, ships might turn south too early and run aground.

But wait a minute. Just how do you build a lighthouse *in* the water?

Engineers sank a wooden frame on the shoal and filled it with stones. They surrounded it with a *cofferdam*, a water-tight box that allowed them to pump out all the water. Then they could pour concrete and set limestone slabs on the exposed shoal.

They finished by adding brick all around. After they removed the cofferdam, presto! They had a strong foundation that rose above the water.

On top of Waugoshance's foundation, called a crib, they built a small keeper's quarters attached to a brick-and-iron tower. Reaching sixty-three feet, it featured a Fresnel lens that could be seen for sixteen miles. Despite its importance, the Waugoshance Shoal Light often found it difficult to retain keepers. You might think that's because it was so isolated, plus the only way to get back and forth to the mainland was by boat—and very often in very rough water.

But you would be wrong. According to local legend, the Waugoshance light is so haunted that keepers didn't want to work there!

A family history recounts the tale of Andrew Davenport, assistant keeper at Waugoshance. In 1883, his wife, Clara, became so scared of mysteriously opening doors and strange groans and creaks that she refused to stay there alone. When her husband went to light the tower, she would climb up there with him, holding his hand the entire way!

Documents tell of a tragedy that happened three years later, to main keeper Thomas Marshall. He was returning home from visiting his family on Mackinac Island on May 28, 1886, when a storm blew in. His sailboat was being towed by a boat with an engine, but in the choppy waters, the propeller severed the line. Marshall raised his sails, but that's the last anyone saw of him. A ferry found his boat the next day . . . *empty.* His body was never found.

Perhaps Marshall's ghost haunts the lighthouse, forever seeking rescue. But others believe it belongs to another keeper, John Herman. He started as a second assistant keeper at Waugoshance in 1887 and worked his way up to head keeper in 1892. He loved to play practical jokes on his assistants, and he once locked one in 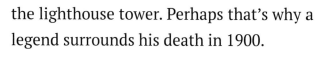 the lighthouse tower. Perhaps that's why a legend surrounds his death in 1900.

As the story goes, he locked one of his assistants in the tower. As the poor man peered over the side and yelled to be let out, he saw Herman on the crib below. He was laughing so hard, he started to stagger around the slippery surface.

Someone else eventually let the angry assistant out of the tower, but when they went to confront Herman, he had vanished. They assumed he had fallen off the crib and drowned.

But it turns out that that Herman actually died while visiting family on Mackinac Island. His death certificate lists heart failure as the cause. We don't know if he got up to trouble while on Mackinac, but that doesn't mean his practical-joking ghost doesn't haunt Waugoshance. Because stories soon arose of a poltergeist—that's what you call a ghost who likes to pull pranks—who kicked chairs out from under dozing keepers. He also liked to slam doors to disturb their sleep, rattle cutlery in the kitchen, and scoop coal into the stove.

So pretty soon, keepers were refusing to take jobs on Waugoshance. Between 1900 and 1912, thirteen keepers resigned or transferred away! And yes, the Lighthouse Board would probably say they closed Waugoshance because they built a bigger, better light nearby at White Shoal. But we all know it was the ghosts, right?

More than thirty years later, the US Navy used Waugoshance for target practice during World War II. Bombs set the lighthouse interior on fire, completely destroying it. Vandals and exposure to the elements gutted the rest of the structure. But in the late 1990s, a local group formed to try to rescue the historic building.

And guess what? The ghost showed up to play tricks on them too. In 2001, one man went out to do some clean-up. He turned around and noticed his boat wasn't where he left it. When he found it, it had been tied with a knot he'd never seen before. As he recalled, "I untied it and got out as fast as I possibly could!"

Good idea!

Another local, a frequent kayaker, found that he had trouble every time he approached the lighthouse. Ice would close in on his kayak, or he would suddenly capsize. On one trip, he finally managed to get one hand on the ladder to the landing. Then "a rogue wave slammed me and my kayak into the lighthouse crib. I floundered like a fish as someone *laughed out loud*."

Perhaps it was John Herman, or another keeper's ghost, not wanting to share his home with the living! And today, the Waugoshance ghost has achieved that goal. Unfortunately, you can't visit the ruined lighthouse. Efforts to restore it have proved too expensive, so it continues to decay. But you can sail past it or see it from the shoreline of Wilderness State Park.

Just don't get too close, or you might become the prankster poltergeist's next victim!

Seul Choix Pointe Lighthouse

CHAPTER 10

The Smoking Spirit of Seul Choix Point

We're going to keep heading west on Lake Michigan, bearing slightly north. At the end of our forty-mile journey, we'll reach the southern coast of the Upper Peninsula. And that's where we'll find the *very* haunted Seul Choix Point Lighthouse.

As you might have guessed from the spelling, the name is French, and locals pronounce it *sis-shwa*. It means "only choice," and legend says it provided the only protection in a storm for some French-speaking sailors. In the 1880s, it was part of a 100-mile stretch of unlit coastline. So Seul Choix was a natural choice for one of the new lighthouses approved for Lake Michigan's busy north coast.

Problems with land, money, and materials delayed construction. But finally, in 1895, the Seul Choix Point Lighthouse opened with a fifty-six-foot tower and attached keepers' quarters. At least three dozen keepers and assistants served the station before it was automated in 1972, but only one became a notorious ghost.

Joseph W. Townshend arrived at Seul Choix Point in 1901, to serve as its second head keeper. He'd transferred from Waugoshance, where John Herman may very well have played practical jokes on him—or even haunted his sleep! (See chapter 9 for that story.)

Herman's ghost wouldn't have followed him to Seul Choix. But Townshend still couldn't catch a break! His wife accompanied him to this post, and she had lots of rules. Number one was NO SMOKING in the house.

This posed a problem, because Townshend enjoyed cigars. So he was forced to smoke them outside, which he did—for the next *nine* years. In 1910, he became the first and only keeper to die at the lighthouse.

Because the place was so remote, his family had to travel some distance for his funeral. (Back then, no bridge connected the Upper and Lower Peninsulas, so travelers had to cross via boat. And remember, there weren't many cars at this time, either. Travel was slow.) So his embalmed corpse remained in the lighthouse basement for *more than three weeks*! Townshend hung around for so long, no wonder his ghost started haunting the place!

Hundreds of reports of supernatural activity have cropped up since his death. But one kind appears over and over: the sudden scent of cigar smoke. The stories go something like this . . .

You're sitting by yourself in an old keeper's bedroom, imagining what it's like to live in a lighthouse. And suddenly, you smell something: the earthy, spicy aroma of tobacco. The smoke burns and tickles your nose. Someone is smoking a cigar in your room!

But no one else is there!

Seul Choix Point Lighthouse is now a museum and has binders filled with hundreds of spooky cigar reports. There are also tales of ghostly figures in mirrors, chairs that move by themselves, and paranormal readings. Some people think there may be three or four other spirits haunting the place, but the best stories connect to Joseph Townshend.

Not only does he like to smoke cigars indoors, but he's also particular about the kitchen. The museum staff have set the table to look as it did when people lived there. And sometimes, they discover that the forks have all been moved. Instead on being on the left side of the plate,

Waves on Lake Michigan

American-style, the forks are set tines-down at the top of the plate, British-style. And who was born in Bristol, England, in 1847? You guessed it—Joseph Townshend!

One last story shows that Townshend's presence extends beyond the kitchen cutlery. In the late 1990s, the museum's alarm went off, notifying staff and police. One officer heard the scraping sounds of a chair on the kitchen floor—but no keeper was living there at the time. After they found no signs of a break-in, they went inside.

A single chair had been pushed back from the kitchen table—Townshend's favorite chair.

But that wasn't the end of it. Two weeks later, the alarm sounded again. Again the police came, and again they found no signs of a crime. But as they drove away, they stopped a bunch of teenagers who were driving toward the lighthouse. The police discovered that on the night of the first alarm, these same teens had broken in to a property nearby. To keep his beloved lighthouse from harm, Townshend's ghost had tripped the alarm!

The Seul Choix Point Lighthouse is still a museum today. You can visit during the summer season, climb the tower, and view artifacts in the museum, including the original Fresnel lens.

But if you smell cigar smoke, maybe it's best not to touch anything—especially the forks!

White River Lighthouse

CHAPTER 11

The Ghosts Who Wouldn't Quit

Put on your life jackets and settle in, we've got a long journey ahead! We're sailing about 150 miles south, toward the harbor of White Lake. Back in the 1870s, during the height of Michigan's timber boom, the harbor became increasingly busy. People were getting rich by turning Michigan's white pine forests into lumber.

Fun fact: during the timber boom, more millionaires lived in the nearby city of Muskegon, Michigan, than in New York City!

And only twenty miles away from Muskegon lay White Lake. Timber companies would cut logs and float them down the White River, which opened into the harbor of White Lake. There ships loaded up Michigan's prized white pine lumber before sailing out into the Great Lakes. The lumber could end up anywhere. Maybe west to Chicago and beyond, via railroads. Or east to Detroit, Cleveland, Buffalo, or Kingston, Ontario.

It became crucial to establish a light station to guide all the ships coming in and out of White Lake. In 1875, Captain William Robinson was given the job of managing the construction of a new lighthouse. The next year, he became its first keeper.

Eventually, he became its first ghost.

Captain Robinson served the White River Light Station for *forty-four* years. He was so dedicated, he refused to retire.

In his later years, Robinson admitted he

could use an assistant—and hired his grandson William Bush. By 1919, the old captain had turned eighty-seven and given most of his duties to Bush. The lighthouse service finally told him he would have to leave.

But the old captain loved the lighthouse too much. On the appointed day, Robinson's friends and family showed up to help him move. Instead, they found him in his bed, *dead*. Rather than give up his home, he had passed away in his sleep.

Since then, stories have spread about how Captain Robinson is still on duty, standing watch over the harbor even after the lamp was removed. People have heard mysterious steps on the stair to the tower. They've seen unexplained flashes from the disused light room. The lighthouse is small, so it's easy to keep track of people. So when visitors see two figures looking out of the tower when no one's around . . . it must be ghosts!

Stubborn Captain Robinson is the most likely candidate, but it might be his wife, Sarah. She spent many years at the lighthouse, raising their children and keeping the property tidy. The lighthouse is now a museum, and its curator swears she has evidence of a helpful ghost.

The curator had found some photos of Sarah Robinson and added them to one of the displays. As she began dusting a glass case, she got called away before she could finish. When she returned, she got a huge shock.

The display case was completely *clean.*

And the dusting rag had moved *to the opposite side of the case*!

The curator tried to get her ghostly helper to dust other cases in the museum, but she had no luck. At least not until a few months later, when she returned to that first room, which had been the Robinson children's nursery. This time when she left the display half-dusted, she came back to find it perfectly clean.

Was this Sarah Robinson's way of thanking the woman for sharing memories of her hardworking lighthouse family? White River Light Station is now a museum you can visit during the summer months. Go there and check it out for yourself.

But take care to wipe off your shoes, so you don't track in any dirt. Unless, of course, you *want* a ghost to haunt your steps!

Lighthouse in South Haven

The Unshakable
Shade of South Haven

It's time to head to our last haunted lighthouse. We'll be sailing south from White River into some of the busiest waters on Lake Michigan. During the 1860s and 1870s, more and more cargo ships hauled Michigan timber across the lake to the big cities of Milwaukee and Chicago. And more and more passenger ships made the reverse journey. Vacationers wanted to escape these hot, smelly, crowded cities and enjoy cool lake breezes on West Michigan's beautiful beaches.

About sixty miles north of the Indiana border lies the port of South Haven. It doesn't have the oldest lighthouse on Lake Michigan (that's in St. Joseph, built in 1832 and located about thirty miles south). And technically, South Haven doesn't even have a lighthouse—it has a light that stands alone at the end of a pier. The keeper's house sat upriver, about a quarter mile away. And that's where we'll find the ghost of one of Michigan's most dedicated keepers.

The first light at South Haven was built at the tip of a pier and began operating in 1872. It could also be accessed by an elevated walkway, which led to a second door near the top of the thirty-foot tower. This long wooden catwalk kept people from being washed off the pier during dangerous storms. In 1874, Captain James Donahue became the light's second keeper.

At first, he served as "acting keeper," since the townspeople might have been skeptical about his ability to do the job. Like many keepers of the era,

Donahue had served in the military. As a member of the Eighth Michigan Infantry, he fought in the Civil War. And at the Battle of the Wilderness in Virginia, he took a musket ball to his left leg. The damage required him to have his leg amputated at the thigh. Donahue walked using crutches or occasionally a wooden leg.

Picture it: a raging Lake Michigan storm brings high winds, fierce rains, and huge waves—yet you must light the lamp. You can't let the gusting winds sweep you away, not when your death could also put sailors in danger! A pail of kerosene hangs heavily from one hand as your other clutches the railing of the catwalk.

Now imagine doing all that *on crutches*.

But that's just what Donahue did. When the winds were too strong, sometimes he even crawled along the path with a lantern gripped between his teeth!

After eighteen months, he'd officially earned the keeper post—and the local people's gratitude.

Shipwreck in Lake Huron

South Haven had no lifesaving station until 1887, so Donahue also had to monitor the shoreline for people in danger.

During his years of service, he was credited with saving fifteen lives—including two of his sons, who needed rescue after they went swimming in deep water off the pier. Local sailors and the federal government gave him medals to honor his lifesaving.

South Haven extended the pier and built a new light tower in 1901. Although it added another 250 feet to his journey, Donahue—now sixty-one years old—continued his dedicated service. He may have had unofficial assistance from his six sons, but he remained the keeper of record until he retired in 1909.

In total, Donahue remained at his post for twenty-five years—and locals believe his spirit is still there. While the light is maintained by the US Coast Guard, the keeper's house has since become part of the Michigan Maritime

Museum. And staff there have heard the creaks and squeaks of footsteps on floorboards coming from the floor above them ... even when they knew *no one was there*.

Maybe it's just the wind coming off Lake Michigan. But then why do doors suddenly open or close, even when all the windows are shut? Why have volunteers heard ghostly voices echoing in an empty hallway? Why have visitors suddenly shivered, finding an unexpected cold spot in an otherwise cozy room?

Sounds like ghosts to me!

You can see the old keeper's dwelling if you visit the museum. Or you can climb aboard one of the Maritime Museum's replica boats—see what it was like to sail a sloop in 1810, picnic on the Black River in 1890, or rescue endangered sailors with the Coast Guard in 1950.

I hope you've enjoyed our lake tour of Michigan's most haunted lighthouses! Hopefully you'll get a chance to see them in person one day. Make sure to take a moment and remember the men and women who devoted their lives to keeping the Great Lakes safe for ships and sailors.

Because if you don't . . . that's when you might hear phantom footsteps, see a shadow behind you in the mirror, or shiver in an unexpected cold spot. Because the ghosts we've met have one thing in common: not even *death* can stop them from telling us their stories.

Diane Telgen is a longtime author and editor of reference books, including *Defining Moments: The Gilded Age,* and holds an MFA in Writing for Children and Young Adults from Vermont College of Fine Arts. Growing up in Michigan, she loved myths and legends about fantastical creatures but was equally fascinated by stories about life long ago. She loved combining both these interests—history and the supernatural—for the Spooky America series.

Check out some of the other Spooky America titles available now!

Spooky America was adapted from the creeptastic Haunted America series, for adults. Haunted America explores historical haunts in cities and regions across America. Each book chronicles both the widely known and less-familiar history behind local ghosts and other unexplained mysteries. Here's more from the original *Michigan's Haunted Lighthouses* author Dianna Higgs Stampfler:

Death & Lighthouses on the Great Lakes

Coming 2022!

www.MiHauntedLighthouses.com